AWAITING
CREATION

AWAITING CREATION

GAIL KADISON GOLDEN

To order additional copies of this book, contact:
Xlibris Corporation
1-888-795-4274
www.Xlibris.com
Orders@Xlibris.com
14913

To my late father, Samuel Kadison,
who gave me music, poetry, and laughter.

To my mother, Anne Kadison Weinstein,
who gave me life more than once.

To my husband, Howard,
whose endless love still amazes, inspires
and sustains me in all that I do.

To the two most beautiful people I know:
my daughters, Rachel and Deborah,
who give me faith in the future.

CONTENTS

Author's Note

There are many people who have made invaluable contributions to this book: Alice Donaldson provided her beautiful way of seeing and her photographs; Phyllis B. Frank helped make the book a reality in many ways; poets Honor Moore and Mary Stewart Hammond taught me craft; the Overlook Terrace Poets helped refine many of these poems; and the Wellspring Women's Writing Collective helped me find my voice.

Sometimes being a poet is a lonely calling. I have been lucky to have the love and support of many people. My brother Ted Kadison and his wife Stephanie have come to almost every poetry reading I have ever given; my aunts, uncles and cousins have been enormously encouraging; my son-in-law James Carlson has honored my poetry by setting several poems to music; my son-in-law Clifford Meade has stood by my side at important times; Fred Workman has always made me feel special; Lynne Sheinkin has shared with me her gift of spirit; and my many friends and colleagues have made my world a very rich place.

Finally I honor my grandmother, Celia Posner, who came to this country as a young girl, and became the matriarch of a large, loving, creative family. Before she died, she asked, 'You will remember Grandma?' as if any of us who knew her could forget.

Prologue

The Woodcarver

(For Nechemyah)

We often ran from the old woodcarver
who sat on broken logs, furiously cutting
at blocks of oak or cherry,
his boots showered with piles of chips.

We fled his stories, which were too long,
his unforgiving eyes,
an accent so thick
spittle flew from his tongue.

Once in a while, we would stop anyway,
watch his slashing knife
birth solemn rabbis in fur hats,
thick-lipped women, goats that smiled.

For this attention, he sometimes gave us
candleholders, cups, figurines.
We hated that his sweat
dripped into the wood.

Today, dusting a long ignored figure,
I was startled by the perfection of each curve,
the well sanded wood, the stories lost
in every deep cut.

I

STORIES RETOLD

Sarah's Response[1*]

"So early next morning, Abraham saddled his ass
and took with him two of his servants and his son
Isaac . . . "

Genesis 22:3

Small wonder that you set upon your way,
even before the sun explored my tent.
You knew I would have questioned
and quickly suspected the horror of your purpose.

What should it mean to me
that some voice in your head
urged you to slaughter my son,
binding him like an animal on the altar?

Every voice in my head
would have shouted madman! murderer!
Who is fit to judge
which of our voices is God?

Men will meet for centuries to come
waving swords in different names,
each tearing the flesh of the other,
with certainty.

_____

*Notes on the Poems begin on page 101.

I do not understand a God that needs this test.
My God bids me feed my child, shelter strangers,
gather in ripe fruits.
Is that not grand enough?

I raised a son with laughter in his eyes.
They are glassy now with terror.
For this I will forgive neither you
nor your God.

I am old, Abraham. Most days
my strength is small. But do not be deceived.
If ever again you raise a weapon to my child,
I will defend him with all the fury in my withered hands.

And who could be so certain
which of us had truly heard
God's voice?

Hagar

"Now Sarai, Abram's wife, bore him no children; and
she had a handmaid, an Egyptian, whose name was
Hagar. And Sarai said unto Abram: 'Behold now, the
Lord hath restrained me from bearing; go in, I pray
thee unto my handmaid; it may be that I shall be
builded up through her.'"

Genesis 16:1-2

Sara, it was you who sent him to my tent,
so great was your shame at giving him no son.
     I never longed for him, his body aging,
     his eyes seeking only his God.
It was you who sent him to my bed.
I suffered vaguely his withered touch.
     Was it my fault that he began to notice
     my dark skin, my long smooth limbs?
I did exactly as you wished. I conceived his child.
Through months of desert heat, aching and swollen
I carried the baby you could not bear.
For this you began to hate me, your hatred growing
as your eyes came to rest on the beauty of my son,
     on Ishmael.

     Whatever did you think,
     that I would not love him?
His birth was a miracle to me as in time
the birth of Isaac was a miracle to you.

My son was magnificent and strong.
I think his father loved him for a while.

Then Isaac came. Of course Ishmael teased.
Your house grew small with two sons.
        Your face spoke hatred for me and my child.
        Your face spoke death.
Abraham turned away, showing Isaac his favor.
Ishmael claimed the power of those who are spurned.
        So I loved him even more
        because he needed me.

Finally you gave us one flask of water,
one loaf of bread and sent us
into the desert to die.
        The wish was yours.
        The words were Abraham's.

For many hours I held my child, parched and burning
but I could not watch him die. When he no longer knew me
I placed him in a patch of shade and walked away weeping.
        In later years your scribes wrote
        that an angel came and helped me find water
        so that Ishmael would live.

Today Sara, I tell you there was no angel,
only a band of travelers who heard my grief,
offered water, and took us to another place
where Ishmael grew to manhood
in anger and in strength.

        Did you wonder or know we had survived?
        Did you once regret your heart's angry mandate?
We often listened for news of you. We heard once
that Abraham took your son to a mountaintop,

tied him like an animal and put a knife to his throat
before some kind spirit stayed his hand.
      I wept for you then though I did not love you
        and do not love you now.
Sometimes when I remember today, there are times when
I weep for us both.

Sara, we never talked. Why was it necessary
that our sons grow with no love for each other?
      The land was endless,
        there were acres enough for many,
        blessing enough for both.

Lost in the wounds and furies of our souls
we did not see the danger,
that while we broke each other's hearts
Abraham would have murdered both our sons.

Waiting for Jacob

"And Jacob said: I will serve you seven years for your
younger daughter Rachel."

Genesis 29:18

In the first year, I could not even pass his tent.
My body hurt, as with some illness,
breasts throbbed to feel the tips of his fingers.
Thin slivers of moon sliced the nights,
I felt its sharp edges tear my dreams with longing.

In the second year, with little rain, we worried for the crops.
I was glad, avoided his eyes when they sought my face,
lost myself, watched skies for clouds,
studied leaves intensely for a hint of wind, a suggestion of death.
Thoughts of moist dark fields filled me with terror.
In the third year, coldness settled on me,
there was little I could feel. No more did music of flutes
urge me towards his tent, watching for his shadow.
Once I joined the dancing but my feet were leaden.

When rose petals fell to the ground, I first saw blood,
looked again, saw a girl's perfumed memory.

In the fourth year, his beard had hints of gray.
His shoulders bent with unseen weights.
At the well, young men smiled, their thick black hair became part
of dark tapestries I saw as I waited in bed, restless for sleep.

By the fifth year, few women of my years had lived without a man,
so I was often called to help with birth, sickness, death.
I came to know others as I had not before,
came to love them better, and myself.

Once at a kinsman's bedside, Jacob whispered that our time
was now in sight. His words were pleasant, his breath stale and sour.
In the sixth year, loneliness had melted in me, no longer a hard cold center,
just warm silence, to hear new sounds in new ways,
to see both sun and shadow on the underside of leaves.

At harvest's end, there was talk of my wedding in one year's time.
The golden round bellied moon lay heavy on all my dreams.

At the end of the seventh year, they came for me in my tent.
My sister wept the tears I only felt. A pale wedge of moon
urged that I recall how the rustle of his coat once burned
between my legs. But when they raised the veils
and placed my hand in his, I found
I could not remember his name.

Rahab

"And it came to pass at the seventh time, when the
priests blew with the horns, that Joshua said unto the
people: 'Shout, for the Lord hath given you the city.
And the city shall be devoted, even it and all that
is therein, to the Lord; only Rahab the harlot shall
live, she and all that are with her in the house because
she hid the messengers that we sent.'"

                                    Joshua 6:16-17

I was afraid when they came to my door
flinging gold on the table,
both demanding to have me.
We had heard of these strange fierce men
whose God taught them magic, parting the waters,
causing the death of kings.
Yet at second glance, they were only men,
alive with passion for their God and for me.

    I am a harlot,
    I knew what to do.

I had spent years watching men's faces,
guessing what they want,
guessing at the range of their power.
I saw they meant to conquer.
    I meant to survive.

When the kingsmen came pounding on the door,
seeking two Hebrew spies, I thought with haste
and hid those two among stalks of flax drying on the roof.
I sent the king's soldiers far afield lying:
'The men that you want are long gone.'
Then I went back to the roof
and asked for my price.

'I know you will conquer my people,' I said
and tossed my scented black hair.
'I have aging parents, I have brothers
and sisters,' I said and turned so my breasts,
which they had each just caressed, stirred their memory
and made them tremble again with pleasure.
'I have hidden you, now will you spare me
and those I love when you come into Jericho?'

They hesitated, I trembled, the moon
took pity and gave my desperation
the color of allure. Then one told me
to hang a scarlet cord in my window
when the city fell. They swore to spare me.
'I will hang the scarlet cord in the window,' I said,
'I will not betray you.'
          I meant to survive.

I gathered my family.
'Jericho will fall,' I told them,
'but we may live because I am a harlot.'

The city fell. Horribly. They spared no one.
The blood of old woman and children in cradles
ran together in the streets, yet
no one entered my house.

Just before they burned the city,
Joshua sent for me and my household.
We watched the flames from a tent
outside the Hebrews' camp.
I wept for my neighbors and the friends
of my childhood but I exulted also
because the flames were not for me.

And so I live out my days.
Some call me heroine, some harlot,
I say neither, only woman like any other,
bartering what we can, what we must.
　　　We mean to survive.

Bathsheba

"When the wife of Uriah heard that Uriah her husband was dead, she made lamentation for her husband. And when the mourning was over, David sent and brought her to his house, and she became his wife, and bore him a son. But the thing that David had done displeased the Lord."

II Samuel 11: 26-27

What should I have done then?
David was the king.
When he commanded me to come, I came,
though I was still grieving
for the gentle husband
who slept in my soul.

Uriah lay with me in sweetness,
David lay with me in power.
Power seduces.

At night I dreamed of clean things,
bathing children, new linen,
Uriah's hand on my breast.
By day I was drugged by the smell of blood,
the sound of my pulse
when David touched me,
when my grief yielded to his majesty.

Who could refuse both a ruler of men
and a singer of songs?
Yet I never forgave him,
even while my body melted in betrayal.

Our first child died, a judgment against the king.
Yet it was my child too.
I wept endlessly for the tiny fingers,
the wondering wide eyes.

Our second child we called Solomon.
Of him it is foretold that his splendor
will last across the ages.
Perhaps this end will forgive the beginning.

Yet some nights, while my king sings songs of glory,
Uriah comes to me as he came, early in our love,
smiling, with gifts of figs, and flowers.
He asks if I remember how he loved me
and I answer him: 'Beloved, I remember,
for it seemed I was a queen then,
as I have not been since,
as I will never be again.'

Ruth to Naomi

Of course I followed after you,
not so much for virtue, as was later written,
but for need and for desire.

At first we were strangers, bound by words only,
some idea of kinship. I did not know your god,
you could not eat my food.
But the days wove themselves about us in seasons,
with patterns we made together,
new plantings, new harvest.
I learned the language of your prayers,
you learned to sing my songs.
Sometimes we shared our work,
drawing water, baking bread.
I learned I could depend on you for simple things.

While the days wove themselves about us,
threads pulling tighter, I came to find pleasure
in your joy, for you did not envy mine.
I learned that, with you, I could also share sadness,
that your comfort flowed strong and real
from fountains of your own pain.

To some I am bound by kinship, ties blood strong.
To you I was bound by days growing numerous,
till once you shared a memory with me,
then I shared one with you,
and it was the same memory.

When the changing moon brought loss and death,
the sun spilled backwards over all the days
that had gone before, and they became more precious,
acquiring a glow I need for my life.

Then I watched you gather your few belongings,
watched your eyes behold me in farewell,
and I said: "I will never have more than I have this day."
So I followed after you, but not so much for virtue,
as was later written.

Yael

"Blessed above women shall Yael be, the wife of Heber
the Kenite. Above women in the tent shall she be
blessed . . . her hand she put to the tent pin and her
right hand to the workman's hammer and with the
hammer she smote Sisera, she smote him through the
head . . ."

Judges 5: 24-26

Though he asked for water, still I gave him milk.
Watching him lift his bowl to thirsty lips,
he seemed a man like others. Somewhere,
an eager woman would wait for his return.

The blanket folded round him, just like any man
and I thought perhaps I could not harm his peaceful form.
I was meant for healing, and the babe at breast,
women's work and kneading hot, sweet bread.

Yet to me were given the instruments of death,
and the wrathful laws of a hard god.
When I saw the hammer there, I took it for a sign,
but now I think it was a hammer, nothing more.

Was I truly righteous, or did I love the power
of his blood upon my hands,
even though it sickened me
and sickens still. Yet I struck.

Better to have held the pillow
to his face and let him slip away.
Better to have called for soldiers,
killing is their work. Yet I struck,

and through the rattle of his death
I heard the songs of praise,
thrilled to be as men were,
triumphant in battle, gloried in song.

But listen, can you hear the song they sing in praise of me?
Can you hear them say "Yael" and again,
"Yael"? Can you hear it, the music,
hammer pounding spike, crushing bone,
the people jubilant, blood oozing,
the song of triumph in battle,
the rattle of his death, my life,
my breath.

Susannah and the Elders

Afterwards, the smell of orange blossoms
always made her ill, perfume summoning memory—
angry voices, cold sweat between her breasts,
waiting to die, stone by stone by stone.

Before that, she and the world
found each other unsullied,
new leaves unfolding and cool mornings,
before the sun scorched memories of dawn.

In her father's courtyard, she dressed in white linen
and servants combed her hair. There were palm trees
for shade and others heavy with fruit,
persimmons the color of flame and citrons pale yellow.

In her husband's courtyard, she dressed
in white linen, and servants combed her hair.
There were palm trees for shade and others
for fruit, dark red pomegranates and oranges.

Bearded rabbis taught her virtue,
hoping to cloister her in commandments,
for her beauty caused men to mutter
as she hurried through market.

In the garden that afternoon, while she washed herself,
the trees seemed to sprout eyes, the birds to caw lewdly.
Then branches became arms
and the trees became elders in black robes.

As the judges accused her, the people gathered stones.
Breathing orange blossoms,
she imagined the first throw,
where it would strike, and then—

the sudden shattering sound
of a man at the edge of the crowd
proclaiming her innocence
with the voice of an outraged God.

And so it ended, but never wholly.
Before, sleep came easy, crescent moons
cradling her dreams. Afterwards, night fell hard,
crushing her with shadowed fears and branches reaching.

By day she walked through burial grounds,
seeking the graves of women dead by accusation.
When she found them, she left flowers, bloodroot and lily,
guessing sometimes God could speak too late.

> *Dedicated to Amina Lawal, sentenced to death by stoning*
> *under religious law, in Nigeria, August 19, 2002.*

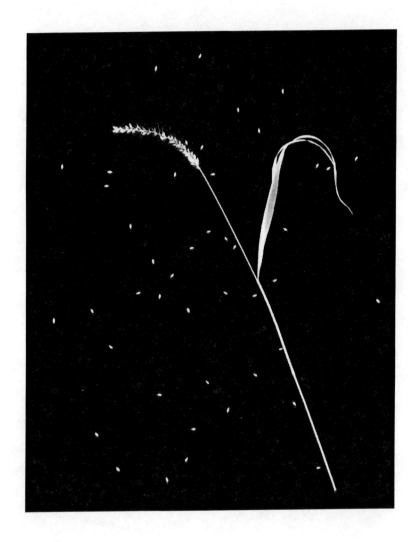

II

Awaiting Creation

Mothers of God

"We are all meant to be mothers of God."
Meister Eckhart (1260-c. 1329)

Mary at the foot of the cross is also rocking
the cradle through soft sweet midnights
while the white music box in the nursery plays
a song over and over again,
a song that can not conclude, only pause
and begin again.

In Delaware, at Rehoboth Beach,
they carve the face of Jesus in the sand,
as the summer throbs
up and down the boardwalk, children
cry for ices, candy, glow sticks,
lovers throw balls at hoops,
hoping to win stuffed unicorns,
the tide moves toward the beach
so that there will be no face in the morning,
so that the face will always have to made again.

Every wound bleeds.
We are drowning in blood.

Children wait at the border
between Turkey and Kurdistan,
shiver on the television screen

while their mothers wrap them in plastic,
but they freeze right through,
all night long, and in the morning are dead.

Mary give us the gift
of your grief.

At Mount Saint Alphonsus, my room
was on the west side of the river.
In the morning I could watch the sun
crown above the mountain on the far side.
Through the stained glass windows
the sun belonged to the fathers in long black robes,
and not to me, but through the tall, narrow
window of my room, the sun
and all the power to bless were mine.

At the border between Turkey and Kurdistan,
a mother wraps her child's body in a shawl and starts
down the mountain over the border for a coffin.
Soldiers raise their guns but she will not stop
and they will not shoot.

Living without armor, everything touches,
Every cloud and shadow, every wind.

We wait at the border
between time and space.
Mary give us the gift of your courage,
to wholly welcome every annunciation
though death is already written
into the angel's face.

We are all meant to be mothers of God,
on the road home from the empty tomb,

when there is no road that we want to walk,
when we walk simply because it is what we do,
on the desolated beach, in the ashes of a star,
in the sudden shadow of our love returned to us,
wounded, transfigured, awaiting creation.

(1990 The Gulf War)

Seed

And what if some of those strange, oddly-titled books are true,
what if he never wholly died that time on Calvary,
but passed out with the heat, the blood, the stink of vinegar—
and they took him down and put him in the cave?

And what if Joseph of Arimathea, tucking him into the cave for eternity,
felt a feather of breath and nursed him in secret for three days
and three nights, so on the third day he went out,
greeted Thomas and slowly kept walking,

thinking of burdens too heavy and wounds too deep,
thinking, it is done . . . the obedience to the hard father,
the mother weeping, and the few who understand
will forget what they understood.

Perhaps he would have made his way to a ship
headed for Africa to find in time, whatever woman,
whatever piece of land, loving to run his hands along both,
feeling grass, hair, flesh and stone.

Maybe he had children, new and easy to love,
but would not take them fishing though he cherished
the cool rivers and the boats going out to sea. And
would sit at evening staring at the fire

and the woman would say 'what is it' and he would not answer,
but had more children who helped him in the fields
where he smiled at tiny green shoots
that broke through the earth.

And if he sometimes would visit the sick,
sitting by their bedsides, they always felt better when he came
but he would make no miracles, remembering
the nails in his hands and his feet.

And maybe he died that second time in bed,
a very old man, safe, warm,
knowing his seed, like Abraham's
would multiply through generations, peopling the earth,

and you pass them every day,
the man who peddles the evening news,
the woman who stops you to ask for a light . . . .

Cana, Without Wine

for Gordon

1

Brooklyn winter,
dancing Jews in long black coats
claim their rabbi as messiah.
I want to lift my feet and dance with them,
longing as they do for miracles.

Over the bridge
in Manhattan, you lie withering
under the sad eyes of a plaster saint.
No prayers redeem your body
from the death some long-ago lover planted.

The rabbi on the balcony
is frailer yet than you.
I want a miracle in time you both can share.
Your days fill with flowers, pink azaleas,
lavender hibiscus. White nurses disinfect your room.

2

Last summer,
there were ribbons, purple, red, blue.
We were laughing on the fairway.
Our tall graying group shared fudge
and popcorn, cheering for parades of sheep.

We guessed
the curliest and wooliest,
clapped for those that won ribbons.
One of us took pictures,
knowing.

3
Spring returns much,
the light of late afternoon, a post card lost for months
under mounds of snow. But you have come
to an end of seasons
in a small western churchyard.

Summer will come
without you, a wedding with no wine.
At Cana, when there was no wine,
Mary asked for a miracle,
though it was not yet time.

4
Visiting your lover,
we stay for dinner. He lovingly slices,
then serves, the eggs
you sealed last summer
in jars of spice.

Summer heat hovers.
I write a poem for you that will not end,
afraid to let you go again. I want
to put my words in jars of spice,
and find them transformed next winter.

At night, asleep,
I bury a friend now dead for thirty years.
Things take time.

Silent on the balcony, the rabbi waits.
On the other side of a river,
I wait too.

Gifts

(for Celia Posner)

She sat amidst
the clutter of her life,
my grandmother,
and packed it
into shopping bags.
Two sets of dishes,
one for meat,
one for milk,
pots, ladles, an iron cocker spaniel
that cracked nuts.

Into boxes, into bags,
she prepared
for the second great migration
of her life.
Once from Russia
to the bowels of New York,
now from Queens
to the beaches of Miami.
Leaving children,
leaving childrens' children,
looking for sun
and extra years of life.

One pot she held back.
'Here,' she said, 'you take this.
it makes good soup. You remember?'
I remembered. During the War,
the army took my father,
my mother took a job,
my grandmother took me.

Frightened at first,
piercing with effort
her thick Yiddish accent,
I slipped into the strange
rhythm of her days.

Fish markets we perused,
(me with a father at war
frightened of so much deadness)
she stared the fish down
like so many Cossacks,
selecting only those
who dared to look back.

We blitzed a dozen shops,
a nickel here, a quarter there,
accumulating feasts
from a handful of change.

My turn at last,
she rested in the playground.
'Play,' she said.
'Children should play.'

Later she cooked:
pots of soups, puddings and fish,
and sometimes I helped.

Then she would share with me
the secrets of her craft,
which seemed to me then
like Kaballah.

At other times,
I did not want to help,
and then she would observe,
'Later, you'll have plenty time to cook,
so now you'll play,
children should play.'

At night, the strange
peach-colored apartment
filled with people
talking of war on faded
couches, waiting for telegrams
in musty halls.

But in the morning again,
we were only two,
marketing through a war,
making a world of playgrounds
and soup pots.

When the war ended
my parents took me
half a continent away
from the peach-colored apartment.
My grandmother cried for weeks.
I was silent
and did not smile.

I never lived with her again.
We always kept in touch-

by letter, by phone, by plane,
in thoughts, in wishes, in dreams.

We still keep in touch,
I still have her pot,
it always makes
wonderful soup.

My Mother's Kitchen

was so vast I could ride a tricycle across the blue linoleum floor,
while always on the table, a small wooden radio played news,
soap operas, Les Paul and Mary Ford.

Unafraid of calories, cholesterol or the shapes of bodies,
we had a deep fryer for chicken, onion rings, donuts rolled in cinnamon
that could stain brown paper lunch bags with lovely dark oil,

and a large oven for cake that could rise to such heights that while it baked
we could slam no doors. In my mother's kitchen, we waited for my father,
who often traveled, to come home.

One February found him in Chicago and we baked him a valentine cake
iced with mocha cream and studded
with red cinnamon hearts.

When snow kept him away for days we licked icing off the edges,
aching to cut the tip off the heart for tasting but
loving him so we kept it perfect.

In that kitchen, the ceiling was covered with rice,
remnants of the pressure cooker that lost its top.
My mother laughed.

In later kitchens, there was not as much space.
We measured the days by my father's heartbeats,
irregular and strained.

The green plastic salt shaker no longer on the table,
we gave the fryer away, ate broiled lean meat,
baked potatoes.

In later kitchens, my mother sweetened black coffee with tiny tablets of saccharine;
spread melba toast with cottage cheese; uneasy with a body that softened
and curved and with my father's heart, beating strange time.

Friday nights and holidays gave again familiar smells of yeast bread
and soup with golden islands of chicken fat, floating,
but we grew careful,

no longer easy in these kitchens which grew smaller with every move.
Still later kitchens saw broiled fish, steamed vegetables, chicken
with no skin. No matter.

After the funeral, we sat around the long dining room table.
The rabbi said we must eat, a sign
that we would go on living.

My mother lives today with a man who cooks for her.
Sometimes we call her for recipes. Last week
after apple picking, we asked about pie.

She remembers everything. How much cinnamon
the apples need, the way
to get a flaky crust.

Ten minutes later she calls again. The real secret, she says, is lots and lots of sugar.
Pour it all over the bottom of the pan, and in time it will rise.
It will sweeten everything.

Stains

Here is the summer—July, 1950.
Heat hangs on us like wet wool,
St. Louis is landlocked,
I have not yet seen an ocean.

Air conditioning exists, but not for anyone we know.
Only the movies have it, cool red seats,
white screens. My mother takes us every night
though the films are lusty.

My father, not with us, lies awake in tangled sheets,
a white hospital gown. At 26 his heart chokes
and sputters. At the end of every film
my mother cries.

Here is the hospital lobby, the sign— 'No Children Allowed.'
My brother and I wait longingly,
my mother pleads with a woman in spotless clothes—
'Sorry, sorry, sorry.'

In an elevator for laundry, behind the back stairs,
we ride unseen with carts of soiled sheets.
I guess the stains are blood.
I am afraid it is my father's.

His deep tan bleached gray, his laughter washed thin,
he welcomes us. The doctors say
he will not live to raise us,
but he comes home.

He takes us East to oceans,
North to pinewoods. For thirty more years,
he tells us each day is a pure gift
and we agree.

Yet, this morning, late for work,
I find myself slowly cleaning counter, stove, floor,
wiping out stains I can never leave alone
and still can not remove.

Harvest

The sign said: 'Pick your own apples,'
and I, heavy with a child as yet unharvested,
came into the orchard, impelled, as if
the sign were a mandate.

The trees and I, clumsy with ripe fruit,
weary beneath a dying autumn sun,
knew each other, sang but one song-

sang, 'This is precious beyond all reckoning,
this moment before the harvest.
I seize it, breathe it, elongate the seconds,
this last moment in which I am
both the tree and the fruit.
I am all, all of it.
It is all of me.'

To let it go, to let it fall away from me,
becoming other, is like a dream,
as it is a dream in February,
to hold a winter apple,
and remember that it comes from trees.

Food for Maria Rosa

1.
Maria Rosa wakes early to catch busses for the gravy-
colored building where
she will visit for an hour with her son.

Morning presses painfully through gated
windows, to play on rows of bottles
she collects for cash.

She fries a pork chop, wraps it in
a wrinkled bag and puts
a paper flower in her hair.

2.
In the gravy-colored building, she sits in a room, behind one-way
mirrors, on a grey plastic chair, and watches her son stack blocks. She thinks
he misses her. She thinks his socks don't match. She thinks he wants
the pork chop she has brought him, though it is long before lunch. Behind
a one way mirror, people watch Maria Rosa watch her son.
The social worker tells her it is not a good idea to look so sad.

3.
On the way home, the foster mother takes away the cold
greasy chop, and the child forgets
if he is happy
or not.

4.
Just a matter of time and they will take the
child away. Maria Rosa thumbs a ragged bible
for some verses that will tell her
why.

She brings the bottles up the road for change-
amber, green, brown or clear, no matter
how they catch the light, each of them
is only worth so much.

Embers

The boy who plays
with matches sleeps sitting up,
like a sentry, fully clothed,
one eye partly open.

Night stalks the house, gnawing on memories,
spitting the remains back into his dreams.

He'd rather be a sailor, keeping watch on deck,
charting his life by the burning light of stars.

But his course is sketched in the ashes
of the burned baby, the black

leaving smudges on his heart,
the way the finger of the priest
leaves smudges on his forehead
at the start of Lent.

Warsaw Pediatrics

for Dr. Adina Szwajger 1918-1993

Just before the Germans came
for the sick children
at the hospital in Warsaw,
she hurried upstairs to her floor,
gathered the children around her,
and told them they must get into their beds.

Hurrying from child to child,
she bent over each small face
and spooned a gentle death
into every unsuspecting mouth.
'This will take away
your pain,' she said.

Who gives absolution
for the pediatrician
of the Warsaw ghetto?
On the first floor she could hear the Germans
pushing children into trucks.
There were screams, and crying.

On her floor there was silence.
She checked them all,
the ones she had saved from starvation

with scraps of stolen food,
the ones she found each day
in the square, orphaned.

Someone has said,
'in the holocaust God hid his face.'
Downstairs she could hear
the heavy step of boots
and children calling 'mama.'
She checked each slack mouth, each still chest
and saw they had escaped.

Roofs That Open To The Sky

Friday afternoon, the Jewess greets the Sabbath
on the steps of a cathedral,
awash in honey gold October.
She is waiting for a priest she has never seen,
but knows from meetings in cyberspace.
Together they will travel to Soho, dine on vegetables,
and then he will lecture on the Tao Te Ching in a room with red brick walls.

In the Hebrew Lunar Calendar, the holiest day has come and gone.
She has neither fasted nor prayed,
but spent the day in the garden revising poems,
calling them out to the trees.
She does not hear the music of the people,
asking to be written in the Book of Life.

At the Feast of Tabernacles, she is not outside
dining in the succot* hung with apples and gourds,
but is straining to hear the soft voice of a Bhuddist monk
whose words echo in the high vaulted arches of St. John the Divine.
Sometimes he rings a bell, for mindfulness,
and the ringing of the bell echoes, echoes, echoes,
high over the nave and she imagines the sounds
ringing out into the night, floating over the tops of the succot,
blessing their roofs which open to the sky,
their poles, which hold up the world.

*ritual booths with open roofs for dining during the holiday

III

Music

Intermezzo

In Aruba the ocean is tranquil, soothing.
I float all afternoon in a haven of waves,
gazing at divi trees, how they grow in the shape of the wind.

People sit at white tables, beneath awnings.
Mornings they sip coffee from Colombia,
afternoons, beer from Holland.

Tiny birds with bright yellow bellies
perch on the chairs and bar stools.
Natives on the island call them sugar thieves
because they wait, singing, to steal sweet crumbs.

I pull a lounge chair under a bamboo hut for shade.
An angry man says I intrude on his space,
tells me to get a hut of my own.

Baby lizards, colors of gemstones,
emerald, aquamarine, play in the sun,
and an enormous green lizard sits very still on a palm,
becoming one with the tree.

In the afternoon the Caribbean sparkles like turquoise glass.
A dark-skinned man trudges barefoot across the sand, smiling.
He helps me find shade, and then
moves on to someone else and someone else.

All day long he drags chairs, often smiling, often singing.
In Aruba, I remember how to perch along the rails.

Marriage Rondo

sometimes the strings are so out of tune it is
hateful and could drive you
crazy and sometimes

I try to tune it up and I wind it so tight
the string breaks and sometimes
the weather is

so contrary that I can't tune it anyway and days
go by when I can't play
a simple scale

because when I wind the string to exactly
the right place the peg
unrolls all

the way back and it just keeps doing that as if
I am destined to never play
another note

and sometimes I want to give it away and play
something else like a drum
or a kazoo

and sometimes I think about what it would be like
to play nothing at all and never
worry again about

tone and tempo and articulation and often I walk by
the living room and just to see it
there waiting makes me

smile and somedays I get every note right and my
god it sings and vibrates through
my body

and my heart and I breathe in rhythm and the birds
outside sing like the dawn
of creation

Nocturne

Yehuda at one in the morning wants
desperately to play Chopin waltzes with
all necessary passion but his landlord
says: 'impossible.'

One friend who tunes pianos has plans—
tiny gloves on the hammers,
a curtain on the soundboard,
something that will muffle.

Key West these July nights is an underworld
of heat, wanting to play Chopin,
waiting for the tuner to dampen
the sound.

And memories of Ruth, who died in long
slow phrases and woke him every
hour all night long, so that now
several years after her death, the art
of sleeping through the night is lost to him.
But not playing Chopin.

Yehuda at 3 A.M. is longing to play
Liszt, the not yet arrived dawn a perfect
setting for arpeggios sighing.

The grey hairs in his beard crackle. He plans
his next concert, considers also his grand-
daughter who at nine is already composing.
He can teach her so much.

At dawn the tuner calls. So *sorry* . . .
forgot . . . *no sleep* . . . . *girl friend not well*
she cries . . . *he cries* . . . *but the piano*
he knows . . . *so vital* . . . *he will* . . .

Yehuda tries to sleep through the worst
of the afternoon heat.
He dreams of women who cry and
the sound of Rachmaninoff played thunderously
on a Steinway grand with the lid
open.

Impromptu

Shabbaz at the piano stretches his small fingers
but can't catch the octave.
Other intervals quickly please his ears.

Last night a snowstorm played crescendos
against snaps of branches cracking. A long
white morning with his father
shoveling my driveway and Shabbaz appears
in my door, hiding from the cold. I ask him in for cocoa
but he sees the piano. There is nothing else he wants.

'I already know how to play that,' he says,
'I can sing you a song,' then he touches
the keys with wonder, singing nothing
with his voice, only with his hands which seek out
pleasing notes, slowly repeating them over and over.

Most five year olds bang but his fingers listen
for the colors of the chords and he is hearing sun
on stained glass. Outside are clicks of sleet, a shovel's clang,
boots thudding up the walk and his father has come for him.
I tell the father Shabbaz has a feel for music and he mutters,
' I don't have money to do nothing for him like that.'

Shabbaz pulls his gray woolen cap far down over his ears.
'Did you like that last song I played?' he asks
and I tell him it was beautiful.
'Yes, it was,' he agrees, 'but sad.
A real sad song.'

Fantasie in B Flat

my brother plays soprano sax like no one else
  the gasping descent of our sled on winter's first frozen hill
    chorus of parakeets darting green and blue across the room
      tat tat tat of marionettes dancing on white dresser tops

a tall Navajo always stood outside my room
  by day he was a dark robed statue
    but night gave him fierce black eyes
      to follow every move

across the hall my brother's room gave shelter
  red and blue balloons floating up from new sheets
    and white curtains   drifting up now
      through his horn

my brother summons spirits   wails my father back into the world
  laughing in outdoor markets   where merchants hawk fantasies coiled
    in small clay pots   and my father dances on dreams
      which become days   then nights   then days again

sliding off the cool notes we cast lines
  in hidden creeks   silent lakes
    our poles heavy with summer days
      the moon mirrored in water   a thousand fireflies

have you ever wanted to play   what stops you
  is it the thin bamboo reed in the mouthpiece
    or the long row of keys   or the people
      dancing far up inside where you can not reach

Cello Suite

prelude

For years I watched from balconies,
backs of auditoriums,
the lawn at Tanglewood,
watched the cellos,

watched the hands
in mysterious dance,
pulsing vibratos
through the halls—

watched motions of bow
define sound.
For years I said
'I should play the cello,'

said it again over lunch with a friend,
heard at last the desire
throbbing between words,
left the diner consumed with intention,

floated through details as if in a dream,
renting the cello, finding the teacher,
climbing the stairs for the lesson at last.
It was easy.

ii

allemande

I am transported by the smell of rosin,
grooved fingers, and the sound
vibrating against me
into my chest,

though I can scarcely endure
the unbearable noise,
Brahms lullaby as it was never
meant to be played.

Summer mornings I practice,
enraged. How dare anything
be this hard. Perspiration
dampens resolve,

shoulders ache, bifocals steam.
My whimsy becomes
a grotesque assault against
all that is beautiful.

iii

courante

Yet I love the tiny, freckled teacher whose hands fly from note to note,
her frayed sweater exuding elegance when she plays,
need how she finds purpose in my confusion,

love Saturday lessons, scurrying up Broadway
balancing cello, purse, umbrella,
feeling invulnerable,

find inspiration in the teacher's room above
a violin shop, a room barely furnished,
but profuse with music.

For months the violinmaker scowls, knows I am an impostor,
unworthy of dusty rooms where instruments
hang from walls, lie on tables, awaiting his strange tools.

Others more skilled confer with him, whisper
over beautiful brown instruments.
I pass through.

iv

sarabande

A friend asks, 'do you still play the cello'
and I say, 'yes but I'm not any good,'
and he says, 'does it matter?'

Another friend and I recall teenage years
when each of us played piano, sonatas glowing
through winter afternoons.

Yet we both stopped, mortified at not being Horowitz
or Rubinstein, or the high school prodigy
who played every assembly.

Capable, with modest talent,
we loved the music enough for a lifetime
and simply stopped.

v

minuet 1

Whenever I practice, the dog seems pleased,
runs for a squeaking toy frog, then chews her noise
along with sounds I torture from strings.

Others in the house play radios, wearily close doors,
and I, sympathetic, still long for a time when people will
open their doors to listen. Why?

vi

minuet 2

I am sounding better. Sometimes
I can close my eyes and find
the right place on the string.

Hands and eyes hear, I feel
sounds, can play longer before
back and shoulders throb.

When autumn brings cool air,
the violinmaker replaces the bridge
on my cello. He no longer scowls.

vii

gigue

I practice in a room with a large window and a mirror.
Just outside, a feeder hangs from the porch.
Birds swoop past, stopping to feed.

The teacher says keep shoulders
down, fingers down.
In the glass I see brown hair, eyes, cello,

feel contorted with struggle,
but my reflection looks serene.
With spring, I reopen windows,

play etudes to an easy breeze.
The birds, seeming to hear,
respond, a feathered orchestra of sound.

Cello song, bird song, spring song,
breathing to music,
I play the morning.

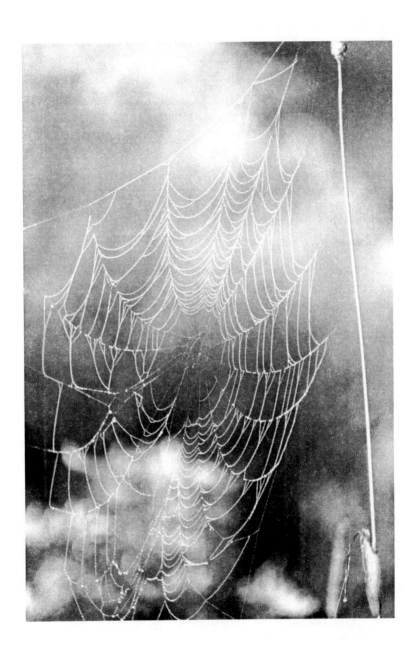

IV

Holding the Shapes Together

Green

She can remember the feel of grass
as if it were the touch of her first lover,
meadow grass, wild, unbounded,
and now so far away it could
be growing on a star.
And the meadow smell after rain,
sweet grass, bluegrass, timothy,
fragrant with earth,
or with leaves fallen all across it, red, gold,
a last gift of color before snow.

She navigates the stroller past rotting orange peels,
dog droppings, here, there,
a syringe. Like a pilot avoiding danger
she plots a course forward
propelled by a longing that quickens
her blood and hurts to remember.
It is August. Even this early the pavement sizzles
and bags of garbage awaiting collection reek.
Crossing streets with numbers,
crossing streets with names,
she fears she will never get there,
fears when she gets there it will not be enough.

A first view of the park by the river and the green eases her,
but coming close reveals rumpled sleepers
coiled beneath the trees, shopping carts,
empty bottles sprouting.

She has come so far, she will stay a while,
the child wants to play. She aches
to tell him of pine woods, tiger lilies, fireflies,
but he is clapping for the pigeons eating trash.

Visions

1.
Last summer on Second Avenue I saw everything—
women with hair the color of ripe tomatoes,
men in white turbans, orange dashikis,
old women with plastic bread bags on their feet,
dogs with raincoats.

That was the summer the doctor drilled
small holes in your eyes.
They thought you might go blind.
I sat in shadows and waited.

On the street it seemed like everyone was swinging way out
to the edge of some invisible tent,
never looking down for the net, just barely holding on.
I described it all for you exactly.

we were ten when you saw me for the first time.
I grew up reflected in your grey-green eyes.

I watched boys with shaved heads
and pierced noses swinging through the evening
and wondered what would happen
if we all let go.

2.
At the foot of our bed the brown lap dog
who has slept there for fifteen years wakes daily
just minutes before the alarm and rouses us.
Mostly blind, somewhat deaf, she nonetheless
greets each day, racing down stairs she can not see,
leaping into laps on faith, sometimes falling once or twice
before the perfect landing is achieved.
The vet says she does not look back
but takes what she needs from the present,
guided by deep memory.

3.
You are part of my deep memory.
The most beautiful picture of me
is the one in your eyes,
which the doctors cut and stitch.
Outside on Second Avenue
violent summer rain floods the street.
Strollers have soaked their hightops,
flip-flops, bierkinstocks.
One or two laugh and go barefoot.

My cousin arrives with carrot juice,
my brother with plums.
My mother rides the bus from Jersey
to sit with me in the dark.
She brings you navy blue pajamas
with maroon piping.
This is the only thing that makes me cry.

4.
What you see first is me,
blurred but clearly recognizable,
like something seen through a window
streaked with rain.
Time will heal the focus.

Outside on the street the storm has spent itself.
Skaters on rollerblades jump puddles.
It looks like someone is going to fall,
but nobody does.

Bones

"Bones Heal!"
This, from the doctor in an elegant suit,
the color of cafe latte.
"In time, the fragments knit together,"
like memories, or dreams.

But the sharp ends of your bones
puncture me in ways I had forgotten
(on the grass with my eyes closed,
the wind sounds likes it is breaking the leaves).

Fragments of your bone float white
in the deep black space of the film—lines—
the trajectory of two cars about to collide,
the blood trickling down your face, into your eyes.

Memories bleed . . . I want to suture them,
grow a thin layer of skin, dulling recall—
a burning smell, a sound of tearing steel.
I touch your arm and feel each metal plate.

An old friend calls: he has had two dreams of me-
in the first, I am in danger, in the second I am safe.
Asleep, my road keeps ending in smoke.

The doctor holds the shiny black film up to the light. He smiles
at the straight, white bone brightening the middle.

Driving at last past the place it happened
I am stunned that it is still beautiful.
The clear Berkshire light casts a gloss on the road,
abundant maples cast shadows.

Everyone is gone—the medics in white shirts,
firemen, a grey-suited trooper. Someone has
swept the road clean. There is nothing left
except the double white line down the middle.

You need to travel on a way before the road changes,
before you're allowed to pass.

Lost[2]

(for Jennifer Harbury)

1.
I dream my husband is lost in the Paris subways again.
Despite facility with maps
and snatches of classroom French,
he cannot find his way above ground.

I am planting trees in a razed country.
In the morning we find each other,
grateful that love comes to us like this
at the breakfast table— easy, familiar.

It is spring and the daffodils instinctively poke through
into bitter weather, never coming to flower.
It is the same spring a woman sits on the long white steps,
day after day, refusing to eat.

2.
Sometimes love comes with a machete slung over one shoulder,
speaking a language that is not our mother tongue,
an uncertain dancer laughing at its own audacity.
After that it cannot stop growing.

Her nightmare was that he would die screaming.
In the empty bed at night she feels the length of his body
strapped to the table, the map of his wounds,
hears the language of questions she knows he will not answer.

What they tell her when she is awake
is that he is lost. She wants a burial
but there is no body and all the tables
are laid with food she cannot swallow.

3.
We only imagine the bodies of the constellations,
holding the shapes together with dots of stars.
She holds his body as an absence, bounded by flickers of memory,
the geography of crushed desire aching on her skin.

Sometimes love comes like a woman seeking the dead,
willing to lose everything, except his bones,
except his bones.

Found Objects

Everyone is looking for the mother of the baby
that was found behind the Exodus Luncheonette
one night after the biggest snow of the year.
It was a dark-skinned baby girl, not a day old,
wrapped in a grey winter coat.
A homeless man, finding the coat,
thought he was in luck, but touching the frozen body,
called for help and the police
took it all for evidence.

Up and down Main Street there are thrift shops
and pawn shops. My neighbor Erin, who collects
antiques, loves to browse in old shops.
She says people have no idea what things are worth.
Last summer the merchants had a sidewalk sale.
I hunted bargains but don't have Erin's eye.
All I saw were chipped cups and saucers, toasters
with frayed cords, jewelry boxes with worn linings.
The dark-skinned baby girl will likely have a satin-lined coffin.
Somebody usually donates one for a found baby.

Our towns have bulk pick up once a month.
You can put anything out. I've seen sofas, tables,
typewriters, lamps. When my friend Pat
was down on her luck, she furnished a whole
apartment by riding around the night before the truck.
Over near Main Street people don't have so much.

At the sidewalk sale, I saw mothers in old flowered dresses
carefully counting nickels to buy their children cotton candy
and puzzles with one or two pieces missing.
Yet, even there, on bulk pick up day, there are always
people rooting through the trash the night before.

Some things are hard to throw away.
I still have my father's eyeglasses in back
of my top drawer, wrapped in his best white handkerchief.
Naturally, they are useless but I am tied by
so many images, such memories.
The dark, frozen umbilical cord was found in the garbage
with the baby, but it could not tie her to anything,
not anything at all.

Ava at Xmas

is pregnant with twins and out on the street.
The babies' father, Santos, would take her
but his mother says no.
Unless they are married in church,
living that way is a sin.
To this he says: 'Maybe when I'm eighteen,
maybe if I find a job . . . '

Last month, the Sisters of Mercy
took her in. Though kindly, they have rules:
'No visitation with men.'
In the hush after midnight, Ava longs
for Santos, who sometimes will hold her
when she's afraid.
This morning she packed.

She could call her mother, but knows too well
the odor of roach spray and wine,
the drunken men
groping late at night.
A call to a shelter and they say, 'Come,
we might find a bed, though at this time
of year, who knows?'

The child she already has, clings
to her hand, shrinking with cold.
He'd like a bed
and is missing the Sisters,
who poured him his milk and tried
to teach him to pray, though he is so small
and some of the words were so hard.

Sister Katherine waters the paperwhite flowers
that grow on her window in bowls of stones.
She prays for Ava,
Ava with petal-frail skin.
'Lord keep her strong. If she can not find roots
in soil, help her blossom
among the rocks.'

The Pink Nude

"Sister Jacques-Marie (formerly Monique Bourgeois) was Matisse's nurse, model and muse from 1942 to 1944. She joined a Dominican convent shortly there-after."

1
memory angles her
pink nakedness on tablecloths
checked blue and white
the artist finding form
hidden in her arms
breasts thighs

heaven is far away
or in the artist's palette
she dare not move
he will paint her
there forever

the pink of her hips
shoulders growing deeper
bordering terra cotta
asking to be touched
everywhere

2
here now there are white
linen habits
cool cloistered walls
prayers cloaked
in silence

pink luminous skin has paled
the languid pose
replaced by genuflection
flesh grown heavy
assumes function
over form

3
'outside the church',
she says
'there can be no
salvation'

Matisse laughs
cuts out
another star

In Darkness

Winter turned suddenly onto Broome Street, claiming December
after many days of sun. In darkness I mistook the numbers and parked far
from the gallery where my daughter helped her friend hang a show.
"Come if you can! It's all women!" she said, knowing how I love to see
what women can create, but now hurrying along cold, broken streets,
I miss my warm suburban den, my half-finished poem.

The right doorway finally, — endless narrow stairs to climb—
ascending leaves me breathless, as does my first look at the explosion
of creation in the bright, narrow loft.
I see strange goddesses come to take me back,
then white panels swabbed with menstrual blood,
then seagrass rendered just the way I dream it.

One artist has painted a rape on a page of The New York Times.
Another gives soft gray lines that make white mantras of space,
and one has written a thousand words in gold,
then painted boats to float on them.

I marvel at a small bronze statue wearing garnets,
and an orange cotton cloud floating in a thin wire coil,
and my daughter, wearing a deep blue dress,
smiling to see that I have come.

Winter[3]

I am wary of the young men who knock at the door
calling for my daughter. I imagine each of them
a potential lord of darkness, come to take her away,
like Persephone, to a grim, barren place where I can not follow.

Will I know his disguise? Some wear three-piece suits,
others flannel shirts and jeans. They are clever.
I allow each one to cross my threshold, serve them bread and meat,
then observe how they hold their knives, use their teeth to tear.

I ask where they come from, mark the speed at which they drive.
As I am vigilant, they are careful.
Is it he of the soft blond curls and angel's face,
he of the ice blue eyes and southern drawl?

Any day now a daughter could vanish
in the arms of some dangerous prince, though I sleep
as lightly as when new babies could wake me
with an awkward breath.

There is little left to do.
I might forbid my daughter
to seek narcissus blooms in open fields,
I might begin collecting snow.

Doubles

October, and every leaf ever fallen spills from baskets,
refusing containment, waiting for wind.
I would need a double to live all the life I want.

In November, three people I know,
who do not know each other,
dream of twins.

Two children appear at the side door, identical but for the hair.
The darker one would come in,
the blond runs to hide.

The desolate brunette at the party weeps into wine,
has been sleeping with the husband of her twin,
has lately been found out.

Tribal elders believed that in sleep a dreamer's double left to wander.
The sleeper was never wakened, lest the double still be roaming,
far from the body.

But what if you and I were startled to wakefulness before our doubles could return?
What if this other climbs mountains in Nepal, beds with strangers,
cuts roses for lovers lost to us?

What if one of us weaves hopelessly through winding streets of a sinister port,
smells death in the morning, makes offerings
to soothe alien gods?

In October we plant bulbs
and burn leaves, perhaps asleep,
dreaming our doubles' return.

The Butterfly Forest

1.
In those years, we had a sleek, gray car—
the nicest one we'd ever owned.
Our two girls rode in the back
and said the ride was bumpy.

We vacationed in the summer when school was out,
and drove to places children would like.
We ate when they were hungry and went to movies
starring girls in pigtails and cartoon mice.

Some of it they remember,
some of it they don't.

2.
At the airport, my daughter meets us at the gate,
glowing with the pleasure of new love, a new home.
We squeeze into the back seat of her car
and she takes us to places we will like.

At the Butterfly Forest we admire the Monarchs,
the Painted Ladies, the Zebra Longwings.
They float around us, land briefly
on a hand, a shoulder, then drift away.

In the center of the room, a glass case holds
rows of chrysalises, about to hatch.
Small opaque sacs
camouflage transformation.

When it's time, they become transparent,
reveal colors, quiver from the struggle to emerge.
My daughter and I watch the way the new butterflies
unfold themselves, lift high above us.

We go off to admire a Queen,
I turn back to see the rows
of wrinkled skins, how
the shapes of caterpillars are no longer visible.

V

CODA

Unfolding[4]

Midway through the book of Chassdic legends,
a child needs help mending.
The story is complex:
the Rabbi tells tales within tales.
I fold back the page, leave
the book on the table, planning to return.
But the tale goes on telling itself.

> *On one rim of space*
> *where the final abyss begins,*
> *stands a fountain.*

At dinner time, the book is moved
to make room for long, yellow ears of corn,
then is forgotten. A few days later
it is found and moved
to a shelf in the den, awaiting summer vacation.

> *On the other rim of space,*
> *where the final abyss ends,*
> *stands the heart of the world.*

At the beach, the book rests on the blanket,
along with towels and jugs of water,
warming in the sun. The children ask the name
of every shell and announce the arrival
of every wave in high voices
I try to memorize.

The fountain is beyond time
and must remain concealed
in the timeless.

At summer's end the pile of reading
is returned to the edge of a bookshelf,
still unread. Months later, I shelve the books
by topic, and then forget.

But from the heart of the world
the fountain receives a temporal life,
for the heart presents it with a day as a gift.

When I remember the book, want and need
to read it, I am living another life,
though the page is still folded
exactly where I left it, twenty years before.
My children are married, my hair greys.

The days flow forth and come to the heart of the world,
and from the heart to the fountain.
and thus the world continues and endures.

The Rabbi tells tales within tales.
The stories are complex.
I open the book.

An Elegy for the Future

1.
In dreams, my mother and I try our hands at writing poems in Yiddish,
a language I never learned and she has long forgotten.

It is a failed effort at some peculiar form of resurrection,
a coda for the clang of oven doors.

> *vas hostu farloren*
> *farloren*
> *what have you lost?*

2.
In Sarajevo, the cellist played a concert in the bombed out square for 22 days,
one day for each of his neighbors, killed waiting in line for bread.
At the close of this century, how many days shall we play our instruments?

> *a rettenish*
> *ich vil der epes fregen*
> *a riddle*
> *I will ask you a riddle.*

3.
Every soul has its mission, said Rabbi Isaac, but often it happens
that the body is taken before the soul is able to finish its work.
And then to achieve its purpose,
a soul may join itself with that of a living person.

shah, shtil
the rabbi will dance again
der rebbe gayt shyn tantzen vider
hush, silence.

4.
Shall I carry some soul with me into the new
millennium? Some spirit deeply known, like
my father, his labors interrupted?
Or one unknown—
an African storyteller lost in the middle passage,
a new mother extinguished at Hiroshima,
a lover, torn from the beloved in Dachau
or Kosovo?

And how would you know if some soul
has come to lodge with you?
Would you dream of hills you have never seen,
hum tunes of unknown origin?

Or carry a great longing that can find no root,
but tangles itself in the minutes and the hours,
a pain with no source?

> *a rettenish*
> *ich vil der epes fregen*
> *a riddle*
> *I will ask you a riddle.*

5.
How shall we move lightly into new time
burdened by the weight of ashes?
Shall we dance with the longing of old bones
which are not ours, but must become ours.

If the world is to be redeemed, Rabbi Isaac said,
every soul must complete its journey.

> *farloren, vas hostu farloren*
> *what have you lost?*

6.
If every step makes the path, where should we begin?
Shall we still sing songs in lost languages,
or do we need a sound as yet unheard,
some pure tone that will ease our way
as we carry each other's souls towards completion,
opening the way to new time
when we will not be afraid of each other

and we will not be afraid.

Notes on the Poems

1 Sarah's Response:
This poem was written for my daughter who wanted to know what I would do if God commanded me to sacrifice a child.

2 Lost:
Jennifer Harbury, an American lawyer, married Efrain Bamaca Velasquez, a Guatemalan rebel leader in 1991. Months later, she was told he had died in battle, but some claimed he was tortured and killed in prison. She mounted a tireless campaign to find his body, to find the truth. In 1995, she at last was told that he had been killed by a Guatemalan military officer on the CIA payroll.

3 Winter:
Demeter was the Greek mother goddess who was responsible for fertility and making things grow. One day, Pluto, the god of the underworld, abducted her daughter Persephone, who was picking wildflowers. Demeter's grief was so great that she stopped everything from growing, causing winter all over the world. She did not allow spring to return until Persephone was returned to her for most of the year.

4 Unfolding:
The source of the Chassidic tale is Martin Buber's *The Tales of Rabbi Nachman*, New York: Avon/Discus Books, 1970.

Acknowledgements

Grateful acknowledgements are made to the following publications where these poems first appeared, sometimes in earlier versions:

"Bathsheba" in *Korone*, Volume 5, 1988
"Cana without Wine" in *Whiskey Island Magazine* #43, April 2001
"Doubles" in *Earth's Daughters*, Fall 1995
"Fantasie in B Flat" in *Karamu*, Spring 1996
"Found Objects" in *Licking River Review*, Volume 32, Summer 2001
"Gifts" in Lesléa Newman, Ed.., *Bubbe Meisehs by Shaynea Maidelehs* (Santa Cruz, California: Herbooks, 1989)
"Hagar" in *The Thirteenth Moon*, Winter 2002
"Harvest" in *The New Jersey Poetry Monthly*, May 1977
"In Darkness" in *Korone*, Volume 9, 1996
"Lost" in *Sojourner, The Women's Forum*, July/August 2000
"Marriage Rondo" in *Fugue*, Number 20, Fall 2000
"Mothers of God" in *Confluence*, September 2002
"Nocturne" in *Confluence*, September 2002
"Ruth to Naomi" in *Korone*, Volume 7, 1992
"Sarah's Response" in *Wellspring*, Volume 1, 1979
"Susannah and the Elders" in *Embers*, Volume XVII, No. 2, 1991
"The Pink Nude" in *Korone*, Volume 8, 1994.
"Visions" in *Eureka Literary Magazine* (forthcoming)
"Waiting for Jacob" in *Visions*, Number 8, 1982
"Warsaw Pediatrics" in *Visions*, Number 43, 1993
"Winter" in *Korone*, Volume 9, 1996
"Yael" in *Korone*, Volume 6, 1990